Julie Davis-Colan   Lee J. Colan

Getting the *BEST* from Yourself and Others

How to Orchestrate Your Attitude

simple truths®
Your Destination For Inspiration

an imprint of Sourcebooks, Inc.

Editing by: Alice Patenaude

Photo Credits
Cover: front, rudall30/Shutterstock; back, Kasa_s/Shutterstock
Internals: page 1, rudall30/Shutterstock; page 6, vic dd/Shutterstock; page 7, Svetlana Prikhnenko/Shutterstock; page 18, Ajgul/Shutterstock; page 20, Kasa_s/Shutterstock; page 22, Martin Good/Shutterstock; page 23, Kasa_s/Shutterstock; page 25, Matthew Cole/Shutterstock; pages 26–27, Darren Baker/Shutterstock; page 37, Kate Swan/Shutterstock; pages 38–39, Andrey Yurlov/Shutterstock; page 42, albumkoretsky/Shutterstock; page 43, Warren Goldswain/Shutterstock; page 46, Martin Good/Shutterstock; page 47, Roman Malyshev/Thinkstock; page 48, Roman Malyshev/Thinkstock; pages 52–53, kwest/Shutterstock; page 55, chatchaisurakram/Thinkstock; pages 56–57, kesipun/Shutterstock; page 60, Route66/Shutterstock; page 63, Horiyan/Shutterstock; pages 64–65, Galina Stepanova/Thinkstock; page 66, EmJcox/Thinkstock; pages 70–71, FWStudio/Shutterstock; page 75, mysondanube/Thinkstock, dapoomll/Thinkstock; pages 80–81, dennisvdw/Thinkstock; page 83, Hollygraphic/Shutterstock; pages 84–85, Marjan_Apostolovic/Thinkstock; page 92, Melpomene/Shutterstock; page 95, Nadezda Razvodovska/Shutterstock; pages 96–97, iremtastan/Thinkstock; page 101, fantom_rd/Shutterstock; pages 104–105, iraua/Shutterstock; pages 110–111, homydesign/Shutterstock; pages 122–123, dwphotos/Shutterstock

Published by Simple Truths, an imprint of Sourcebooks, Inc.
P.O. Box 4410, Naperville, Illinois 60567-4410
(630) 961-3900
Fax: (630) 961-2168
www.sourcebooks.com

Originally published in 2005 in the United States of America by CornerStone Leadership Institute.

Printed and bound in China.
LEO 10 9 8 7 6 5 4 3

"Everything can be taken from a man but one thing: the last of human freedoms—to choose one's attitude in any given set of circumstances, to choose one's own way."

—Viktor E. Frankl

Orchestrate

(ôr'·kǐ·strāt)

To arrange or control the elements of,
as to achieve a desired overall effect

Your Attitude...
reflects your past,
describes your present,
and predicts your future

Contents

Introduction

How do *you* measure success? Is it by financial security, career growth, community involvement, quality of relationships, spiritual centeredness, or the legacy you leave? Whichever measure you choose, your attitude is the single most important factor in achieving success.

The topic of attitude can be conceptual and confusing. In fact, as we go through life, we often hear phrases like "keep your chin up," "look on the bright side," or "you need a winning attitude." Unfortunately, we seldom know how to convert these soft sayings into hard results.

This book translates the incomprehensible into the actionable. It is intended to provide you with inspiration *and* application so you can orchestrate your attitude—and your success.

The great news is that even in the worst situations—as a victim of a natural disaster, prisoner of war, target of abuse, or when you are hit by a string of unfortunate circumstances—**your attitude is something you can always control!**

When we control our attitudes, we influence how our body responds and performs. Where our thoughts and attitudes go, our bodies follow. For example, blushing is a physical reaction to a mere thought. If we have this kind of reaction to a thought, is it such a leap of faith to believe that we can orchestrate our attitudes to affect our bodies in beneficial ways?

In fact, a positive attitude can buffer us against some adverse health effects and depression. Researchers who studied 839 patients over a thirty-year period found a link between optimism and lower risk of early death. Specifically, optimism early in life predicts good health later in life.

Additionally, a landmark study shed light on the ultimate benefit of a positive attitude. In this particular study, **participants who were more positive lived an average of ten years longer than the other participants.** Considering that smoking has been shown to reduce life expectancy by five and a half years for men and seven years for women, your attitude might be a health risk factor worth paying real attention to.

The choice of attitude is yours. So read on, and choose to get the best from yourself and others!

Tomorrow you will become what you choose today.

Aspects of Attitude

You are the conductor of your own attitude!
Nobody else can compose your thoughts for you.

Attitude: Concept or Concrete?

H ave you ever thought about what makes you say things like "that guy has a great attitude" or "boy, her attitude is really killing the team"? How do you know if someone's attitude is great or crummy? When most of us hear the word *attitude*, we think of a fuzzy concept that somehow makes us happy, sad, content, or frustrated.

It is difficult to measure and manage a concept, but it's easier to manage and measure behavior. That's why we will use a broad **definition of attitude: a relatively stable and enduring way to behave.** This definition and the following explanation are designed to help you translate this concept into concrete behaviors that we can easily manage and measure.

How Do Attitudes Develop?

Our attitudes develop from repeatedly thinking, speaking, and acting the same way, over and over, until it becomes a stable and enduring way we behave—a habit. Although we can hear and see our attitudes in the words and actions we choose, attitudes start developing with our thoughts.

Our minds are our ultimate personal computers! What we program into them determines how they will function. The most powerful computer ever made, programmed with the wrong software or with bad data, will never function to its capacity. For instance, just as we have viruses (bad data) in today's cyber world that cause computer malfunctions, our mental computers are also susceptible to the data we put into them. If we choose to load them with bad data, it will limit how effective or successful we will be.

Our attitude is our personal boomerang to the world— whatever we throw out will come back to us. Express enthusiasm and it comes back. Offer a smile and it is returned. Start to gossip and that's what we will hear. Get frustrated with a team member and that's what we will see. Help a colleague and we will find a helping hand. This boomerang effect holds true for our thoughts about money, relationships, self-worth, a performance goal, team building, a problem colleague or customer, a new project or career.

So, once we develop a habit of choosing a positive or negative attitude, that is exactly what we will send to and receive from the world.

Choice: Reaction or Response?

The power of choice is one of the greatest gifts we are given. Although we make many choices every hour of the day, we rarely make neutral choices. Each choice has a positive or negative consequence for us at some level.

Our attitude toward life is the most important choice we make! Let's look at why such a simple choice—embracing a positive or negative attitude—is more challenging than it appears for many people. The bottom line is that we often forget that we have the power to choose. We relinquish it subconsciously, because we make thousands of decisions daily—about 95 percent of them are subconscious.

Just think of the last time you were in deep thought about your plans for the evening while driving home from work. As you pull into your driveway you wonder to yourself, "How did

I get home?" The car seemed to practically drive itself. Driving is a relatively complex task, requiring many choices along the way— turn right, turn left, slow down, stop, change lanes. Still, driving home can be successfully performed almost subconsciously. So, consider the multitude of much smaller choices we make each day that we don't really think about: waking up, brushing our teeth, saying "good morning" to a colleague, eating our lunch, performing a repetitive job duty, and so on. Subconscious actions are useful most of the time, but we must also consciously choose our attitude to control our results.

Our ability to choose is a gift, but it is also a huge responsibility. No matter what today's "it's not my fault" culture encourages, we are all ultimately responsible for our own choices. In fact, we like to write the word *responsibility* as *response— ability.* As humans, we have the unique ability to respond. It is a choice we make, although many times it's an instantaneous or subconscious choice.

Here's a scenario repeated daily. Family dinners are important at the Smith house. Jim and Jane Smith and their two children (John, age three, and Janie, age four) just sat down at the table. Before the first bite of dinner is enjoyed, John spills his milk and it goes everywhere.

A *reaction* to this event: "Not again, John! Every time we eat, this happens. Think, son, think! Do you want to eat in your room from now on?"

A *response* to this event: "Uh-oh, John. Let's get a sponge and clean this up so you can eat your dinner."

When you *react*, you make a purely emotional and subconscious decision. Often, because of how your experiences and prior choices have programmed your subconscious mind, your reactions do not help you achieve the best results.

On the other hand, when you *respond* to a situation, you make a constructive and conscious decision. That's why there are emergency response teams, not emergency reaction teams:

> ♪ When you simply *react*, your emotional instinct is in control, with little thought of the long-range consequences.
>
> ♪ When you *respond*, your brain is fully engaged and your self-awareness is high. You have the long-term consequences in mind.

We all experience plenty of negative situations and people. The key is to be prepared to consciously respond to these negative inputs. Choosing to respond instead of react helps us positively orchestrate our attitudes—and our lives.

A Script for Orchestrating Attitude

There are three aspects of the script that work in concert: thoughts, words, and actions. By orchestrating each aspect with conscious responses, we positively influence our beliefs, commitments, and results.

ORCHESTRATE YOUR...	TO POSITIVELY INFLUENCE...
Thoughts...	Beliefs
Words...	Commitments
Actions...	Results

Orchestrating Attitude Script

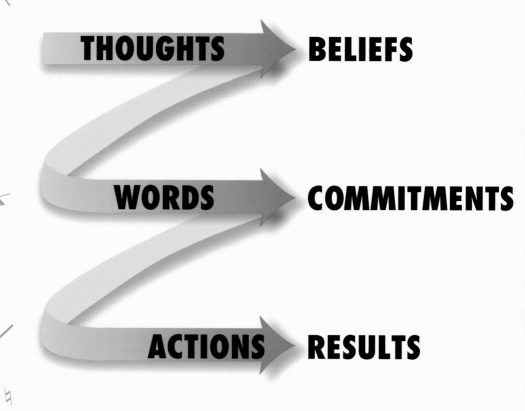

THOUGHTS → BELIEFS

WORDS → COMMITMENTS

ACTIONS → RESULTS

This script is self-reinforcing, for better or for worse. The results we achieve reinforce our thoughts and the same script is played out again. So, it all starts with our thoughts. **Our thoughts today influence our results tomorrow.**

The left side of the script is the side of *choice*. Each of us chooses our thoughts, words, and actions either consciously or subconsciously. Therefore, we influence the right side of the script—the side of *responsibility*. We must take responsibility for our beliefs, commitments, and results. We are each responsible for the choices we make and the results we ultimately achieve. The ultimate choice is ours—victim or victor?

The script plays out like this:

♪ **THOUGHTS**, the way we choose to interpret our world, directly influence our beliefs.

♪ **BELIEFS** directly influence the words we choose to speak to others and, more importantly, to ourselves.

♪ **WORDS** reflect our commitments to ourselves and others.

♪ **COMMITMENTS** influence our choice of actions.

♪ Our **ACTIONS** directly influence the **RESULTS** we achieve.

To illustrate how this script plays out, let's say you are given a new project to lead. You are confident that the prospects for this project are positive and start thinking about how to ensure its success and measure the benefits of the project deliverables. You also think about your talented project team, knowing they will need to go above and beyond to meet the project goals. Your kick-off email contains words like *excited*, *opportunity*, *talented team*, *creative solutions*, and *positive impact*. Team members speak and react in kind, "boomeranging" your winning attitude back to you. Meetings are crisp, roles are clearly defined, and decisions are made collaboratively, yet quickly.

The expected challenges, even the seemingly big ones, are handled professionally and swiftly because the team knows that failure is not an option. Your thoughts and words have already predisposed the team to acting in alignment with your expectation of success. And your eventual success predisposes you to the same thoughts, words, and actions on the next project. This is when the powerful, self-reinforcing script will be played again.

Orchestrating attitude creates a beautiful human symphony. The result is a person of integrity who gets the best from himself and others.

Let's take a closer look at each aspect of the script.

"The greatest discovery of my generation
is that a human being can alter his life
by altering his attitudes of mind."

—William James

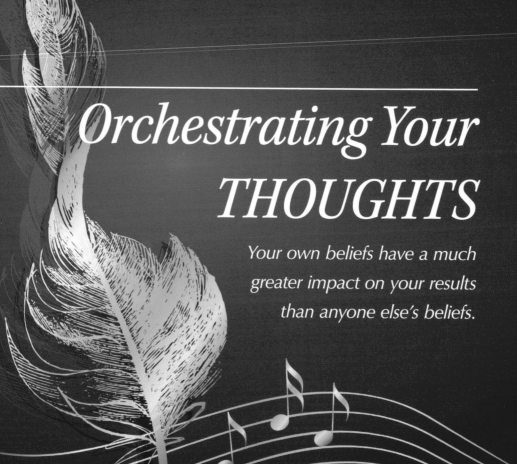

Orchestrating Your
THOUGHTS

Your own beliefs have a much greater impact on your results than anyone else's beliefs.

THOUGHTS ➤ BELIEFS

Our thoughts and beliefs have incredible power to shape our lives and the lives of others. Unfortunately, life is not fair. We don't always get what we deserve. The good news is that **we receive what we believe in life.** This law of life works just as powerfully with negative thoughts as it does with positive ones.

Some people ask, "How can I be positive all the time when negative situations are a reality—they just show up in everyday life?" Yes, bad things do happen, and they sometimes "just show up." However, **it is our interpretation that makes a situation negative.** A situation doesn't drag us down; the way we think about it does.

Like it or not, your thoughts and interpretations of circumstances directly influence your beliefs and, ultimately, your actions. Henry Ford said, "Whether you think you can, or you think you can't—you're right." In other words, **what you think is what you get.**

The great news is that **you** are in control of what you think! No one else has this power unless you give it away. You are the conductor of your own thoughts.

Let's take a look at three instruments for orchestrating your thoughts and think about them!

1. Choose your view.
2. Check your focus.
3. Control your inputs.

Choose Your View

Our experiences are much less important than how we choose to think about them. The way we interpret our experiences shapes our beliefs about the past. Furthermore, our interpretations either limit or enable our future success. For example, a mission-critical project you are leading has "promotion" written all over it, but it bombs—it's over budget, past its deadline, the works. How you choose to interpret those facts is where you can shape your future. Are you a failure, a poor leader who is maxed out and maybe even in over her head? Or, are you a great leader in the making who is learning some tough lessons that will help ensure success on the next project, when your true colors will show? Facts are facts, but the view you take is your choice.

Think the best ALL the time. What's the harm? If you choose to protect yourself from disappointment by always thinking the worst, you have also chosen disappointment as the filter through which you view all things and people...and that's just what you will get. On the other hand, you can choose to think the best all the time. Sure, you might be disappointed occasionally, but, most of the time, you will be programming your mind and others to achieve their best.

If you find yourself having a negative thought, say "STOP!" out loud, and replace it with a positive thought. Saying "STOP!" is important so you can actually hear yourself controlling your own thinking. Let's see how it works.

A friend told us about a situation that used to drive him crazy. He would drive home through rush hour traffic after a hard day and find the driveway to his garage impassable, blocked by his children's bicycles and toys. He *reacted* something like this: "These kids have no sense of responsibility. They never pick up after themselves, and it's a hassle for me to move their junk just to get in the driveway."

Then he said, "STOP!" He decided to choose a more positive view, and he *responded* with, "My children are still just kids. It looks like they had a great time today. Boy, how time flies... I had better seize the moment."

Sure, the driveway still looked like a yard sale after a wind storm. **Nothing changed except his interpretation of the facts.** He substituted gratitude for anger and changed his mind for good.

When you change the way you look at things, you change the way you see them.

The same opportunity to choose our view presents itself many times daily.

Lee and I recently experienced such an opportunity. We were running late for our flight and parked the car in the expensive infield lot to save time. After sprinting into the terminal, we came to a complete halt at the security checkpoint. Getting through security with only ten minutes until departure time, we wove our way quickly around people and courtesy carts. We passed our favorite frozen yogurt stand (oh, the price of running late!) and rushed up to the gate—to be greeted by a sign reading "Flight 619 to Denver departs 8:55 p.m." Delayed *three* hours?!

Lee felt his blood pressure rising and had a desire to *react* to the situation. Fortunately, we had been discussing this topic, so he caught himself and said aloud, "STOP!" (He didn't shout the word, but it was certainly audible enough to turn a few curious heads). That's all he needed to prevent an unproductive reaction. Instead, he *responded* by replying to some emails, reading a chapter of a book he brought along, and writing a little of the book you are reading. Then, he made a few phones calls to reconnect with some friends and checked in with his mother in Florida.

A few minutes later, we saw a well-dressed man doing the same high-speed approach to the gate. He threw his briefcase on the counter and said, "Did the plane leave yet?" The agent pointed to the sign behind her and said, "No, I am sorry, sir. It has been delayed." He *reacted* by barking out, "I am a platinum-level member in your frequent-flier program! Let me talk to your supervisor!" He proceeded to berate the supervisor and furiously make calls on his cell phone. It was understandable that he wanted to try to catch another flight, but he even treated the people on the other end of the calls rudely. His tantrum went on and on with the same apparent lack of results. We lost interest once he started repeating his routine. Guess what time the plane left? 8:55 p.m., still three hours late.

The facts of our situations appeared to be the same, but this man boarded the plane still fuming. We're glad that we did not have to sit next to him! Not only was he late, but he also spent three hours unproductively. Lee had a bounce in his step. The bottom line was that Lee chose his view and was getting the best of himself, while this gentleman was letting the situation get the best of him. We certainly do our share of reacting. This particular situation just happened to highlight the benefits of responding.

Choose a positive, productive view. Create your view inside

out by starting with your thoughts. Don't let your circumstances obstruct your view. When you choose your view, you will always have a clear line of sight to being your best.

"Nothing in life is
so hard that you can't
make it easier by the
way you take it."

—Ellen Glasgow

Check Your Focus

The things we focus on create a magnet for our lives. Focus on opportunities, and doors seem to open. Focus on problems, and obstacles are plentiful.

Have you ever wondered why some people seem to have all the luck? Maybe you are one of the lucky ones. In general, lucky people get the best of themselves and others by focusing on:

Forgiveness	vs.	Anger
Others	vs.	Self
Opportunities	vs.	Problems
Gratitude	vs.	Envy
Abundance	vs.	Scarcity
Today	vs.	Yesterday
Building up	vs.	Breaking down
Humor	vs.	Drama
Controllable things	vs.	Uncontrollable things
Giving	vs.	Taking

The more you focus on the "positive side of life," the more you will attract these things. Focus on forgiveness, and you will find the world forgiving. Focus on the comedy life offers, and your life will be full of laughs. On the other hand, focus on the drama life offers, and your life will be a soap opera.

The truth is that being lucky doesn't have much to do with luck at all. **The most successful people create their own luck by constantly checking their focus.** They appear lucky because their focus has put them in the right place to make good things happen. In other words, luck is 90 percent preparation and 10 percent opportunity.

Looking at how you spend your time, money, and energy is a foolproof way to check your focus. **Time, money, and energy are precious resources—*your* precious resources.** They are finite. When you spend them in one place, you cannot spend them someplace else. To check your focus, look at how you spend your time, money, and energy. Is it mostly on the right- or left-hand column of the chart on page 40? Your answer will tell you if luck is in your future.

"If you want to be happy, put your effort into controlling the sail, not the wind."

—Anonymous

Control Your Inputs

Remember, your mind is your ultimate personal computer. Like your laptop at home, sometimes you might forget to turn on your mental virus protection program, allowing negative thoughts to invade your mind—without you realizing it. So, the computer adage "Garbage in, garbage out" as it applies to your mind should really be "Garbage in, garbage stays."

Your mind never sleeps. You can't pull a "fast one" on it. **Whatever your mind hears from others, and especially from you, it records and stores.** The mind doesn't discriminate between input that is good for you or harmful to you—it collects *all* input. If you hear something often enough, you will tend to believe it and act upon it. Your mind can be your greatest ally or your worst enemy. Seek positive inputs and you will improve your chances of producing positive outputs.

We draw into our lives what we constantly think about— good or bad. If you are obsessing about what your boss will do if you make a mistake, then guess what's likely to happen? If you are always thinking about why you can't seem to get a break, or when the next shoe will drop in your relationship, or what will happen if you can't afford to pay for your car repairs, or why you don't get as much recognition as your colleague, then you are programming your mind (and those around you) to turn these thoughts into your reality. Negative thoughts are land mines along the pathway to being your best.

Fred Smith was a student at Yale when he submitted a paper about the impact of a computerized society and the changes

he envisioned for traditional distribution and delivery systems. Smith's professor returned the paper commenting, "The concept is interesting and well-formed, but in order to earn better than a 'C,' the idea must be feasible." Just five years later, Smith figured out a way to make it feasible and named his company Federal Express. He controlled the input from his professor and others and chose to seek out more positive input.

Consider three of the most common influences that can program us daily. They have the potential for a positive or negative impact on our thoughts and, ultimately, our results.

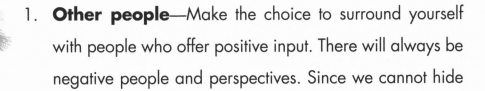

1. **Other people**—Make the choice to surround yourself with people who offer positive input. There will always be negative people and perspectives. Since we cannot hide

from them, we must learn to filter out negative input to minimize "garbage" in our thoughts. The best strategy is to make a conscious effort to *get to know and spend time with people who have a positive outlook.*

2. **Media**—The subconscious mind is most receptive five minutes before we doze off at night, a common time for watching the news. Unfortunately, much of the news today shows the worst side of people and the world. When you hear a news story, remind yourself that news often follows the adage "if it bleeds, it leads." Doing so will help you balance potentially negative input with more uplifting thoughts.

So how can you remain well-informed and maintain a positive outlook? *Monitor what you watch.* Make the choice to watch programs that are more educational, artistic, spiritual, or sports- and comedy-oriented. These types of programs stimulate positive thoughts.

Many people, particularly in the business world, start their day reading the news. Before you start reading, take a quick inventory of all the things you have to be grateful for. Additionally, make it a habit to *finish your reading with an inspiring story* so your mind is primed for a positive day.

3. **Yourself**—No one is with you as much as you are! You have an opportunity every day to consciously give yourself positive input and reinforce your own positive actions. In fact, Julie has a practice of giving herself mental high fives. That is, she frequently tells herself,

"Great job, Julie!" We each talk with many people each day, but *the most important conversation is the one we have with ourselves.*

The three sources of input listed above have the potential for a positive or negative impact on your attitude and, ultimately, your results. Take a look around you. Are you controlling your inputs?

Here are two powerful, yet underutilized strategies for controlling your inputs:

1. **Read books and listen to podcasts.** Did you know that the average person spends five hundred hours a year in his car? Capture that time by listening to audio books. Choose your reading content to flood your mind

with positive input. Simply reading one hour a day for two to three years will make you an authority on a topic, while feeding your mind with positive thoughts.

2. **Practice visualization.** Control your inputs by not only visualizing your goals, but also imagining exactly how your body feels when you achieve your goal. Your mind does not know the difference between physical and mental practice. Visualization is the process that allows you to see your desired results in your mind. Once you can see it in your mind, you'll be closer to achieving it in your life.

You are what you think,

SO CONTROL YOUR INPUTS!

"*We become what we think about.*"

—Earl Nightingale

Orchestrating Your Thoughts— Application

What is your single biggest challenge or problem?

What are three positive things relative to this challenge?

Considering the three positive points above, restate your challenge as an opportunity you would want to embrace.

Now, start using this new description to think about your opportunity!

Orchestrating Your Thoughts

1. Choose your view.

2. Check your focus.

3. Control your inputs.

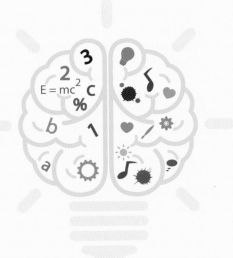

You are who you are today because of what you believed yesterday. You will become tomorrow who you believe you are today.

Orchestrating Your WORDS

Whether said in love or anger, gratitude or envy, your words leave a lasting impression.

WORDS ➡ COMMITMENTS

Remember the old saying "Choose your words carefully"? This phrase is used to warn the speaker of the impact of her words on others. In reality, the greater impact is on the speaker, not the receiver. Once you have spoken or heard the words, they become programmed into your mind. **It's not what you say, but what you *repeatedly* say.** The words you repeat are gradually convincing your mind that these statements are true, therefore precluding your mind's eye from seeing any possibility to prove your words wrong.

Our mind hears our words, good or bad, and then programs our brain accordingly. We will likely prove ourselves correct if we find ourselves consistently saying:

♪　I don't deserve this.

♪　I can't do that.

♪　I will never be that successful.

♪　I will never get the great assignments.

♪　I just have bad luck.

♪　I can't win unless someone else loses.

♪　I will never get out of this mess.

Words reflect our commitments to act. **Our words tell the truth.** Whether we have a long conversation with a friend or a short interaction at work, every word makes a difference. The results of our interactions are rarely neutral; they are almost always positive or negative. Ask yourself, "Do my words reflect a commitment to being joyful, helping others, creating 'win-wins,' keeping things in perspective, seizing the moment, continuously learning, embracing change?"

Words are the seeds of commitment. We plant the seeds with each movement of our lips. Once they are spoken, our words either grow in the form of an immediate response or they take time to germinate. Whether the result becomes apparent sooner or later, we cannot speak words of failure and defeat and expect a life of success and victory.

Here are three instruments for orchestrating your words:

1. Talk yourself up!

2. Speak with strength.

3. Ask the right questions.

"One person with a commitment is worth more than a hundred who only have an interest."

—Mary Crowley

Talk Yourself Up!

D id you know that you talk more to yourself than to anyone else in the world? In the face of challenging situations (and we all have our share), the words you choose for that conversation with yourself will directly impact how long you will find yourself in those situations. **Use your words to *change* your situation, not to describe it.** The moment you speak something—good or bad—you give birth to it as an idea, an expectation, a desire. You have planted the seed that will, sooner or later, grow into the results you will reap.

When you're feeling somewhat down, don't tell people how you feel; tell them how you *want* to feel. By controlling what you say and how you say it—using positive words with enthusiasm—you help to change your physical and mental state.

We remember the year we started our business. We jokingly refer to it as "the year we told a million lies" because we spent a lot of time talking ourselves up.

Like most start-up businesses, we had our share of challenges, disappointments, and adjustments. Many well-intended friends asked, "Hey, how's your business coming along?" We could have described our situation by saying, "Gee, it's been a tough year. We have had to really dig into savings to keep things going, and it's been a lot harder than we thought it would be to convert existing business relationships into paying customers. To boot, it's a lot more work than we thought it would be."

That type of response would not only drag down our friends— and no one wants to hang around a downer for too long—but it also would have planted the seeds of doom for our business. Instead, we chose to use words to change our situation. It wasn't telling a lie; it was simply choosing our view when we responded, "We feel good about our prospects and are confident that we are doing the right things that will pay off long-term. Most importantly, we are passionate about the work, and that's a victory in itself." Although we were far from perfect in consistently responding this way, we are confident that our words planted the seeds of success.

Most people enjoy working and living with people who live and work with a positive, upbeat attitude. **Tell people how you *want* to feel, and it won't be long before you do.** So, the next time you are feeling gloomy and a friend asks how you are doing, talk yourself up!

"Act the way you'd like to be and soon you'll be the way you act."

—Leonard Cohen

Speak with Strength

The words we use are more powerful than we can imagine. Most people greet each other with words that have no power or energy. Think of the last time you heard someone else (or even yourself) respond to a greeting of "How are you?" with "Oh, I am doing so-so," "Hanging in there," "I'm surviving," or "Not too bad." It probably wasn't much past yesterday.

Now, try this experiment. The next time anyone asks, *"How are you?"* whether it's someone at work or a cashier at the store, respond with strength. Give them an energetic, enthusiastic "Great!" or "Terrific!" It will be hard to do without a smile on your face, and you are likely to get one back. Second, you will likely feel a physical response of increased energy. Third, your words will send a message to your mind that will be consistent with feeling *Great!* or *Terrific!* To see the results, you have to do this often and with sincere enthusiasm (not robotically). When you do, your subconscious mind will begin to act on what you are saying and begin to design your reality to be consistent with your thoughts and words.

Speaking with strength also creates a sense of accountability and commitment to get the best from yourself and others. Your challenge is to consciously avoid using words that are strength killers. These words sap energy and commitment from your interactions and, ultimately, your actions. **Eliminate these words from your vocabulary:**

♪ I can't	♪ I don't have the time
♪ If	♪ Maybe
♪ Doubt	♪ I'm afraid of
♪ Try	♪ I don't believe
♪ I don't think	♪ It's impossible

But omitting these negative words is not enough. A sports team needs more than just a good defense to win; it also needs a strong offense. So, you must also mobilize your own offensive assault with the words you choose. **Build positive mental connections, personal strength, and commitment by using these strength builders:**

♪ I can	♪ I will make the time
♪ I will	♪ Positively
♪ Expect the best	♪ I am confident
♪ Commit	♪ I do believe
♪ I know	♪ All things are possible

The power of your actions is preceded by the power of your words. Choose to speak with strength and watch the power of your words bring out the best in yourself and others!

"*Do or do not.*
There is no try."

—Yoda

Ask the Right Questions

T he fastest way to change the answers you receive—from yourself and others—is to change the questions you ask. Consider the possible responses to questions like these:

 What happens if I fail at this?

How will I deal with this problem employee?

How can I get through this situation?

How will I ever afford the car I want?

On the other hand, think about the responses that positive, more empowering questions will yield:

♪ What's the best way for me to be successful at this?

♪ How can I support the success of this employee?

♪ How can I make the most of this situation?

♪ What are the options I need to consider to buy the car I want?

In the last question about affording the car you want, asking the right question opens one's thinking to alternatives like: looking at a used model, no-money-down financing, increasing savings for the next six months to afford the down payment, or looking at leases.

Asking the right question gets you better answers, whether you are asking it of yourself or of others. **The questions you ask will either limit or expand the possible responses you get.** Additionally, your choice of words will dictate how involved, receptive, and motivated the recipient will feel.

For example, in the heat of a month-end deadline, a sales manager might ask his lead representative, "Why are we falling short of this month's sales goal?" The representative naturally feels defensive, put on the spot, and unable to respond to the supervisor's satisfaction, regardless of the reason. An alternative question could be, "What do you think we can do to ensure we meet our sales goal?" Now, the representative feels involved in the solution (versus being accused of the problem), receptive to brainstorming alternatives, and supported by the supervisor. In short, he feels motivated to meet the goal.

The power of the answers you receive is directly proportionate to the power of the questions you ask. Consider how the questions you ask, both at work and at home, elicit certain responses. Ask yourself, "How can I ask questions to get the best from myself and others?"

"*It is not the answer that enlightens, but the question.*"

—Eugène Ionesco

Orchestrating Your Words— Application

What are the five words or phrases you frequently use when communicating with your team, family, or friends?

What do these five words say about your team, family, or relationship?

Which words of strength can you use to substitute for any or all of those you listed above?

Orchestrating Your Words

1. Talk yourself up!

2. Speak with strength.

3. Ask the right questions.

"Your day will go the way the corners of your mouth turn."

—Unknown

Orchestrating Your
ACTIONS

"If you don't make things happen
then things will happen to you."
—Robert Collier

ACTIONS ➡ RESULTS

I n the last chapter, we discussed how positive, powerful words create commitment for your actions. In this chapter, we will address the aspect of attitude that proves your commitment to your words—your actions.

Life rewards action! But even greater rewards await those who orchestrate *positive* actions. For example, while he was still relatively unknown, actor Jim Carrey wrote a check to himself for $10 million for "acting services rendered." As Carrey later explained, it wasn't about money. He knew that if he was making that much, he'd be working with the best people on the best material. As they say in Hollywood, the rest is history.

Life's rewards—loving relationships, meaningful work, financial security, time to relax, leaving a lasting legacy—come to those who *act* to bring them about. Although life isn't always easy, and there are plenty of excuses <u>not</u> to be our best, **the rewards go to those who let their actions rise above their excuses.**

Sometimes our actions get lost in our intentions. Have you ever heard someone say, "I intended to tell her how important she is to our team before she left" or "I intended to volunteer last weekend" or "I meant to vote this past election" or "I intended to keep my commitment, but...?" The truth is, **we judge ourselves by our intentions, but others judge us by our actions.**

If you have practiced the instruments for orchestrating your thoughts and words, your actions will naturally be aligned with your commitments. The result—a positive person of integrity who is getting the best from herself and others!

Now, let's move on to the three instruments for orchestrating your actions:

1. Have a need? Help someone succeed.
2. Move through adversity.
3. Stay connected.

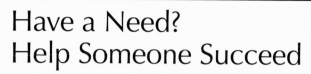

Have a Need?
Help Someone Succeed

When we have a need, we might obsess and continually focus on that need. Maybe it's a financial need or a need for recognition, love, a new challenge, or companionship. We are typically drawn inward by our need with the hope that we can somehow come up with a way to meet it. However, our inward focus often turns into a spiral of despair, and we quickly find ourselves consumed with worry. This is actually a self-absorbed spiral, not to mention a futile one.

So, the next time you have a need, help someone else succeed by asking the right question. Instead of asking, "What's in it for me?" ask the WIIFO question: **"What's in it for *others*?"** Get your mind off of yourself and direct your actions toward someone else. If you find yourself feeling discouraged, volunteer at a hospital or cheer up a friend who is lonely. If you are looking for a job, help someone else with their job search. **If you want to get the best *from* yourself, first give the best *of* yourself.**

Helping others not only helps you shift your focus outward, but also stimulates feelings of gratitude. There is nothing like a dose of gratitude to pick us up. Most importantly, **meeting others' needs brings out our true spirit—it reflects our positive human character.**

But here's the caveat: if you expect something in return for your help, your act of kindness is really an act of trading favors. Be a giver, not a trader.

Mike Haynes is a stellar example of someone who applied this instrument to orchestrate his actions. Mike had been an innocent bystander when a fellow college student went off the deep end and sent bullets flying. Mike was hit.

He was rushed to the hospital, where his heart stopped during surgery. Mike's mom remembers lying next to his hospital bed on a cot, praying more than sleeping, for nights on end.

Once Mike was finally able to leave the hospital, he made a life-changing decision for himself and many others. He decided to change his college major from accounting to rehabilitation, so he could help others. Despite needing assistance himself, Mike soon began helping others who, like him, rely on wheelchairs as a way of life.

Today, you will find Mike at some of the most challenging triathlons. He manages open-water swims, rigorous bike courses, and equally taxing runs.

He is also a nationally ranked tennis player. Mike's passion is working with others who are recovering from injuries and accidents. He loves to coach wheelchair basketball teams, volleyball teams, and those participating in individual sports. He also helps athletes prepare for the Paralympics. Mike had a need and now helps *many* others succeed.

The help you give others is an important part of the legacy you leave. If you don't know where to start, look close to home or work. If a colleague has a Little League game he needs to attend, pick up his load so he can leave early to get to the game. If a neighbor is not feeling well, buy an extra take-out dinner on your way home from work. If a friend is struggling with a relationship, lend an ear. If a young new employee is having trouble adjusting to a new company, offer to show her the ropes. **Help is not help until it is given, so turn your intentions into *acts* of help.**

"We make a living by what we get,
but we make a life by what we give."

—Winston Churchill

Move Through Adversity

A dversity is not reserved for daytime soap operas. Even the most fortunate of us has experienced adversity of some type: job loss, health problems, failed relationships, disappointments at work, financial difficulties, death of loved ones, etc. We intentionally used the word *move* in this instrument. Since adversity has an uncanny knack of paralyzing us, it becomes critical to keep moving through it. Otherwise, we will be stalled in the grip of our adversity. Here are three specific actions to help you move through adversity.

1. **Take inventory.** When we experience a loss, we tend to think all is lost. Identify what is lost or changed and what is not. Then, express your gratitude for what still remains. An attitude of gratitude creates happier, more resilient people. In fact, more and more studies show that gratitude is the most common characteristic among the happiest people.

2. **Convert turning points into learning points.** Use your adversity as a time to pinpoint opportunities to improve, learn, grow, rebuild, or test your own character or faith.

3. **Plan for the future, but live for the present.** Don't obsess about yesterday and don't be seduced by the promise that tomorrow will be better. Our favorite poem says it best:

Yesterday is history,

Tomorrow is a mystery,

Today is a GIFT,

That's why we call it
the PRESENT.

—ALICE MORSE EARLE

"It's not having what you want;
it's wanting what you've got."

—Sheryl Crow

Thomas Edison, the creator of over one thousand inventions, was an optimist who saw the best in everything. His experience serves as a perfect example of moving through adversity. It took Edison one thousand tries to find the right materials for the incandescent lightbulb, but he didn't see them as failures. With each attempt, he gained information about what didn't work, bringing him closer to a solution. Finally, Edison never doubted that he would find the right materials.

By the time Edison had reached his late sixties, the lab he had built in West Orange, New Jersey, was world famous. He called the fourteen-building complex his invention factory. Its main building was massive, larger than three football fields. From that base of operations, he and his staff conceived hundreds of inventions, developed prototypes, manufactured products, and shipped them to customers. It became a model for modern research and manufacturing.

Edison loved the place, but on a December day in 1914, his beloved lab caught fire. As he stood outside and watched it burn, he is reported to have said, "Kids, go get your mother. She'll never see another fire like this one."

Most people would have been crushed. Not Edison. "I am sixty-seven," he said after the tragedy, "but not too old to make a fresh start. I've been through a lot of things like this." He rebuilt the lab, and he kept working for another seventeen years. "I am long on ideas, but short on time," he commented. "I expect to live to be only about a hundred."

Move through adversity like Edison did, and you will light your own pathway to success!

"When one door of happiness closes, another one opens; but often we look so long at the closed door that we do not see the one which has opened for us."

—Helen Keller

Stay Connected

The strength of our relationships is perhaps the greatest measure of the quality of our lives. It is also a key predictor of our sense of internal joy and contentment. **We should act and give our best to our relationships.** They are built on two-way streets and must be mutually beneficial; each person must bring something of value. Otherwise, our relationships will not endure.

There are many ways to stay connected, including professional and personal interest groups. These groups are important, but a few strong bonds play a pivotal role in staying connected and orchestrating your actions.

An excellent way to stay connected is to **build your own BEST team—Buddies who Encourage Success and Truth.** Take some time to think of people who have made a difference for you and for whom you have made a difference.

Choose wisely who you want on your team. Ensure they offer the energy, truth, and positive perspective you need to orchestrate your actions. There is no better test than time when it comes to relationships, so start small and build your BEST team slowly. The key is to connect with your BEST team, individually or as a group, on a consistent basis.

Depending on the relationship, we can play the role of teacher and/or student. In either role, we all need people who will support our success.

Your BEST team can help you:

♪ Move through adversity. They can help ensure you go through the three steps on page 99.

♪ Hone your self-awareness. Depend on your team to give you truthful, constructive feedback to keep beliefs based in reality.

♪ Affirm that your thoughts, words, and actions are aligned with your goals.

♪ Provide a chance to help them. As the Proverb says, "In teaching others, we teach ourselves."

♪ Combat negative input you might receive at home or work.

♪ Rehearse challenging situations with friends before you have a live performance.

Your BEST team is a personal and powerful way to ensure you stay connected and orchestrate your actions.

Orchestrating Your Actions— Application

I dentify just one need you currently have.

Now, who is someone you know who has an even bigger need?

What is one small helping gesture you can offer this person?

When will you do it?

How do you think this will make you feel?

Orchestrating Your Actions

1. Have a need? Help someone succeed.
2. Move through adversity.
3. Stay connected.

"*No dream comes true until you wake up and go to work.*"

—Unknown

A Final Note

A life filled with positive attitude is also filled with positive impact.

Orchestrate your attitude to get the best from yourself and others!

TO ORCHESTRATE YOUR...	PRACTICE THESE INSTRUMENTS...
THOUGHTS	Choose your view. Check your focus. Control your inputs.
WORDS	Talk yourself up! Speak with strength. Ask the right questions.
ACTIONS	Have a need? Help someone succeed. Move through adversity. Stay connected.

You cannot always control your feelings, but you can control your thoughts, words, and actions.

The Power of One

Getting the best from yourself and others all starts with...

ONE Thought
ONE Word
ONE Action.

"One" is the first note in orchestrating your attitude. Contrary to the lyrics from a classic rock song, one is *not* the loneliest number. It's the most important one!

Your thoughts, words, and actions are like individual notes that work in concert to create the power of one person—YOU—to make a difference. You can harness your "power of one" if you simply:

♪ catch one negative thought and turn it into a positive one,

♪ think of one thing for which you are grateful at the beginning of each day,

♪ say one "Fantastic!" when a friend asks how you are doing,

♪ assume the best in one upcoming situation,

♪ keep on moving when you experience adversity, or

♪ help a friend or colleague during a time when you need help.

Some people feel that one vote in an election can't really make a difference. Recent elections decided by razor-thin margins have proven them wrong. **A single act does make a difference... It creates a ripple effect that can be felt many miles and people away.**

Susan Komen's life provides a current day example of the power of one. When Susan was diagnosed with breast cancer in 1978, little was known about the disease and it was rarely discussed in public. Before her death at thirty-six, Susan asked her sister, Nancy, to do everything she could to bring an end to breast cancer. Although Nancy wasn't sure that she alone could accomplish this goal, she kept her promise. In 1982, Nancy established the Susan G. Komen Breast Cancer Foundation with two hundred dollars and a shoe box full of names.

In 1983, the first Susan G. Komen Race for the Cure was held. It attracted eight hundred participants and raised several hundred thousand dollars. At the time of this printing, there were over 120 races globally with 1.6 million participants and over one hundred thousand volunteers. The Race for the Cure has now invested more than $2.2 billion in helping to eradicate breast cancer and has become the worldwide leader in the fight against this disease. In fact, the five-year relative survival rate for women diagnosed with early stage breast cancer has increased from 74 to 99 percent. It all started with one request to one person who took one action.

All great things start as one small thing.

Life Is Your Performance

There are no dress rehearsals for the performance we call *life*. **We get one chance to perform our life's symphony.** No one delivers a perfect performance. We can all expect to miss a note or two, but we should all strive to learn, grow, and improve. Being our best is more about the journey than the destination.

There are plenty of critics in the world, but don't let them stop you from delivering a performance that makes a difference. Remember, you are the conductor of your own attitude.

Did you know that the bumblebee should <u>not</u> be able to fly? Based on its size, weight, and the shape of its body in relationship to the total wingspan, a flying bumblebee is scientifically impossible. The bumblebee, being ignorant of scientific input, goes ahead and flies anyway and makes honey every day. Ignore the sting of negative inputs and thoughts and replace them with positive ones. If you do, you will be able to achieve things that no one else thinks is possible!

Helen Keller was a human bumblebee, and she is a great example of getting the best from herself and others. For the first seven years of her life, she was locked in a world of blindness and deafness where there was little human interaction. With the help of her own BEST team, which included her teacher, Anne Sullivan, she found a way out of her silent existence and into the real world. Like the bumblebee, Helen overcame her limitations and eventually graduated from college. She went on to become an author, a highly sought-after speaker, and a respected and powerful advocate for the blind and deaf around the world.

That's a life performance filled with positive attitude and positive impact—the kind we all want.

Play the first note in your symphony today! Start orchestrating a more positive, powerful attitude. Attitudes don't change overnight, and they certainly don't change by accident. It's your choice. So practice your instruments and *you* can be the one to:

♪ expand your team's creative problem solving,

♪ build a more trusting relationship,

♪ enhance your household earnings,

♪ overcome a fear,

♪ create a defining moment for a needy youngster,

♪ make your community safer, or

♪ build the confidence of a struggling team member.

One note at a time, one instrument at a time—orchestrate your attitude and you *will* get the best from yourself and others!

"Nothing can stop the man
with the right mental attitude
from achieving his goal;
    nothing on earth can help the man
with the wrong mental attitude."

—Thomas Jefferson

About the Authors

Julie Davis-Colan cofounded The L Group Inc., a consulting firm serving leaders since 1999. She is a strategic marketing and organizational health expert. She has been the vision behind The L Group's more than one hundred proprietary products that equip and inspire leaders at every level. In addition, she coauthored *Stick with It: Mastering the Art of Adherence.* Her passion for leadership and life creates an infectious energy for everyone with whom she interacts.

Lee J. Colan, PhD, is cofounder of The L Group Inc. He is an executive consultant and speaker. Lee was nominated for the *Thinkers50* Award for best management thinker globally. He has authored twelve popular leadership books that have been translated into ten languages, including the bestselling *Engaging the Hearts and Minds of All Your Employees: How to Ignite Passionate Performance for Better Business Results* and *Stick with It: Mastering the Art of Adherence.*

Learn more about The L Group by calling
1-972-250-9989 or visiting **www.theLgroup.com**.

The L Group equips and inspires leaders at every level with:

Consulting: Our top-notch consultants deliver cut-through-the-clutter insights that deliver results.

Speaking: Engage your team with passionate delivery and equip them with practical tools.

Executive Advising: Our advisers help executives boost organizational, team, and personal performance.

Resources: Rapid-read books, ready-to-use PowerPoints, training kits, audio programs, leadership assessments, note cards, and posters.

Training: Use our just-add-water training kits for internal delivery or rely on our certified facilitators.

Contact The L Group at 1-972-250-9989 or www.theLgroup.com.